The Round Barns of Winona County, Minnesota, and Environs

The Round Barns of Winona County, Minnesota, and Environs

Round Barn

- Bill Holm - from his book *Landscape of Ghosts*

She and I go to an old round barn by the river.
The barn is full of old hay.
Wind whistles through missing shingles in the high dome.
Iron stalls are empty now.
We see hoof prints on black dirt, made by cattle long since dead
and eaten. From a nail she takes down a horse harness, leather dried and cracked.
"From Iceland," she says, and caresses it.
We walk into the empty hayloft, fifty feet high, shaped like a
cathedral dome. The last sunlight blown into the holes in the dome
by prairie winds shines the floor like a polished ballroom.
I walk under the dome, open my mouth, and sing - an old Italian
song about the lips of Lola the color of cherries.
The sound rolls around the dome and grows.
It comes back to me transformed into horse's neighing.

The barn is gone now, its lumber recycled and its old cattle yard growing soybeans. But the countryside wherever you are will still provide a curious old barn or two for you to visit when your life presents the need. Old barns are fine places for singing, for contemplation, for love. If, in old age, you grow crotchety and awkward, and some snarly young attendant snaps at you, "Were you born in a barn?" smile sweetly and answer, "Yes, me and all the other gods . . ."

1

The Round Barns of Winona County, Minnesota, and Environs

Dedication

This book is dedicated to the American farmer, past, present, and future, especially those in Winona County, Minnesota ~ and even more so, those with round barns.

The Round Barns of Winona County, Minnesota, and Environs

Artist: *Jim Heinlen*
Author: *Larry Kirch*
Picture captions: *Jim Heinlen*
Proofreader: *Sister Eileen Haugh OSF*

© Copyright 1998 Jim Heinlen and Larry Kirch
First Edition
All rights reserved. No part of this book may be reproduced or transmitted in any form or by any means, electronic or mechanical including photocopying, recording or by any information and storage and retrieval system without the express written permission of the aforementioned Jim Heinlen and Larry Kirch.

Library of Congress Catalog Card Number: 98-61572
ISBN: 0-9667816-1-9

Cover: *The Rupprecht Round Barn by Jim Heinlen*

Published by

The Round Barns of Winona County, Minnesota, and Environs

Acknowledgements

All paintings in this book are original works by Jim Heinlen, mostly painted in the late 1970's and early 1980's. Some paintings are recent and depict their condition today. Paintings were graciously supplied from the collection of St. Mary's University, Winona, Minnesota, and are on display at the Fitzgerald Library located on the campus of St. Mary's University. The Michael Kirch barn painting is from Larry Kirch's collection of Jim's work. The original architectural drawings of the "Small Barn" are courtesy of Mr. Robert Wolter, St. Charles, Minnesota. The photographs of the Michael Kirch barn under construction and the Russell Church barn are courtesy of the Winona County Historical Society Archives. The poem "Round Barn" is reprinted with permission from *Landscape of Ghosts* by Bill Holm, Bob Firth and Voyageur Press. The poem "The Round Barn" is reprinted with permission from *Poems for Every Day* by Edna Lovelace, Bertha, Minnesota. The photograph used for the Gallagher barn was furnished by Angela Gallagher Dumond of La Crescent, Minnesota. The Pfeiffer-Dabelstein barn construction photos were loaned courtesy of Sheila and Cliff Murray. The barn photo of the Hans and Louisa Schott round barn near The Arches park was loaned by Daryl and Susan Schwantz. The barn storm damage photograph of the Kalmes barn was kindly allowed by the Winona Daily News. One Pfeiffer-Dabelstein painting was loaned by Dennis and Ellen Bergler, and the oil painting by Jim of the Kalmes farm was courtesy of Betty Acheff. The photograph of the Ames-Marx farm is by Patricia Heinlen Britt. The poem "This Old Barn" is by Joan Murphy and is used with her permission. The Rupprecht barn painting with the cardinal bird in it was courtesy of Joan and Jerry Beier. *Let Barn Tell Whole Story*, courtesy of Marguerite Brogan.

We are also very grateful to all the round barn farmers and their wives, Susan Kirch, Nora O'Dea Heinlen, the Gordon Gerdes, Rose Peshon, the George Fritzes, Betty and Roy Meyer, Jack and Pat Lucas, Patricia Condon Johnson, Harriet Poss, Captain Ron Larson, Shirley Willard, President, Fulton County Historical Society, Round Barn Museum, Rochester, Indiana, Deborah Miller, Minnesota State Historical Society, Ms. Lorry Erickson, Regional Editor of *The Country Today*, Brother Louis DeThomasis, FSC, Brother Roger Chingas, FSC, Dr. Mary Fox and Bob Kierlin for their kind assistance, cooperation and encouragement.

Jim Heinlen and Larry Kirch

The Round Barns of Winona County, Minnesota, and Environs

Foreword

In their chapter on "nonorthogonal" barns in *Barns of the Midwest*, Keith A. Sculle and H. Wayne Price say that round barns are now valued only by "weekend motorists, agricultural sentimentalists, and round barn hobbyists" -- a judgement that is regrettably true. Hailed early in the 20th century as the wave of the future, round barns lost their usefulness as a result of economic and technological changes in agriculture, and now the few that remain--disappearing fast--survive mainly as architectural curiosities. Their esthetic value is widely recognized, and may guarantee the preservation of a few round barns here and there, but these will provide only a hint of the many that once dotted the Midwestern landscape.

Winona County is believed to have had at least twenty-three (twenty-two are documented) round and polygonal barns at one time, placing it at the head of round-barn counties in Minnesota, and in a class with Vernon County, Wisconsin, Stephenson County, Illinois, and Fulton County, Indiana, as one of the premier round-barn counties in the nation. Of these possible twenty-three, only six remain standing in 1998 in Winona County.

Jim Heinlen here offers paintings of twenty round barns--a selection from the wealth of paintings he has done of barns in Minnesota and neighboring states. Seventeen of these are Winona County Barns; the other three are from just across the line in Fillmore, Olmsted, and Wabasha counties. Eight of the barns were standing in 1998; the rest have been razed, blown down, or burned, one as long ago as 1926. Whether already gone, or doomed to be lost in the future, these barns will all live on in Jim Heinlen's masterful paintings.

Roy W. Meyer

Professor Emeritus of English at Minnesota State University, Mankato, Meyer has been photographing and studying round barns since 1966, and is the first and probably the only one to document all of Minnesota's round barns.

Introduction

Round Barns

Although it is not really known who built the first round barn, it is thought that the Shakers built them in Massachusetts in the 1820's. It is said that they built them so that spirits would not hide in the corners. Another possibility is that they were patterned after the Native American wigwams. Still another theory is that they were patterned after the railroad roundhouses which were widely in use in the 1820's. For farming purposes, round barns became popularized by the agricultural land grant colleges such as Purdue University, University of Wisconsin and the University of Illinois. It is known that the barns could be built faster and cheaper since they contained less wood because of the balloon frame structure. It was thought that a farmer could get more hay storage in a round barn than in a rectangular barn and at the time many were built, hay was taxed so the farmers thought that their taxes would be less if they had a round barn. They were also thought to be more efficient since all the cows faced the center and could be fed more quickly (especially if the barn contained a silo). Cleaning was another story since the round barn had a circular gutter. The barn was difficult to retrofit for a barn cleaner as well.

The body of knowledge has been well established about the origins of round and polygonal barns for farming purposes. Many books give a full treatment of Orson Squire Fowler's "A Home for All," which popularized the octagon house. Elliott W. Stewart is said to be the first theorist and Franklin H. King, a professor of agricultural physics at the Wisconsin Agricultural Experimental Station, promoted round barns as an agricultural scientist (as noted in *Barns of the Midwest*, "a biography of King should be written"). Wilber J. Fraser from the University of Illinois Agricultural Experimental Station was also a theorist and promoter. Most barns were designed and built by national "architects" and builders such as Benton Steele and Horace Duncan.

While there are numerous "barn" books that mention round barns, there are only two published works that are entirely devoted to round barns and specifically put them in the historical inventory format, one on Indiana titled *A Round Indiana: Round Barns of the Hoosier State*, by John Hanou, Purdue University Press, and one on Iowa's round barns titled *Without Right Angles: The Round Barns of Iowa*, by Lowell J. Soike, Iowa State Historical Department. These books provide a similar format on the "phenomena" of so-called "round, polygonal, experimental, or nonorthogonal" barns which is followed by a photographic inventory of the barns. In fact, most books on barns contain a chapter on round barns and briefly summarize this information (especially the Shaker barn in Pittsfield, Mass., and George Washington's barn).

Vernon County, Wisconsin, (approximately 50 miles southeast of Winona, Minnesota) has promoted their 16 remaining round barns (Larry Jost reported 21) by preparing a driving tour brochure, and Fulton County, Indiana, also had 16 round and polygonal barns at one time. Winona County has not received much (if any) recognition in the literature for its 22 round barns. Stephenson County, Illinois, has been documented as having had 24 round or nonorthogonal barns. These barns were built by the Shaffer-Haase team that is also known to have built three round barns near Albert Lea (*Barns of the Midwest*, Noble and Wilhelm). Local builders such as the Wolters, Johnsons and Arnoldys should be added to the literature. In addition, national builders may have also built barns in the area.

Of the millions of barns built in this country, the total inventory of round and polygonal barns in the United States is thought to have been 1,048 (*Barns of the Midwest*, Noble and Wilhelm). The estimate for Minnesota is 170, the same as Iowa (*A Round Indiana: Round Barns of the Hoosier State*, John Hanou).

Winona County Round Barns

While there are several publications on barns and round barns in the Midwest, there are no published works about Minnesota round barns. Jim Heinlen and Roy Meyer are the only persons to visually document Winona County's round barns and their historic significance.

Based on research done to date, Winona County, Minnesota, is one of four counties in the United States that had a significant concentration of round and polygonal barns. All barns are being lost at an alarming rate but as round barns are extremely rare, the loss is even more striking. In Winona County, of the 22 (and possibly 23) original round barns, only six remain. There is little remaining opportunity to document this subject in a manner fitting to its importance in Minnesota's history. Many of the remaining barns are slowly losing ground to the ravages of time. As farming practices change, these barns are less likely to be maintained since they are not cost effective.

There was speculation that many of Winona County's round barns were built by a Kansas barn-building company. Yet with local builders such as the Wolters, it is likely that local contractors and not national builders constructed the vast majority of the area's barns. When Jim Heinlen began painting round barns it was thought that there were 16 in total. With additional research, another six have been discovered including the John Small barn in St. Charles Township, the Joe Killian-Jacob Johns barn in Wilson Township, the Martin Gallagher barn in Pleasant Hill Township, the Oscar Bundy barn in Winona Township, and the Hans Schott barn near The Arches in Warren Township. A final barn is thought to have existed on the George Roth farm in St Charles Township. The existence of these barns is noted below in more detail.

John Small -- St. Charles Township
This barn was located approximately one mile north of St. Charles, Minnesota, on the east side of Highway 74. The barn was built by Frederick Wilhelm Wolter of St. Charles and was destroyed by fire.

Joe Killian - Jacob Johns -- Wilson Township
This barn was located on the south side of Winona County Highway 21 approximately 1 mile east of State Highway 43 and one and one half miles north of Interstate 90 (approximately five miles from Winona) near Wilson. This barn is thought to have been constructed around 1908. It was destroyed by fire in 1918. It is thought that Mr. Johns was burning potato vines in the spring and a west wind caught some straw on fire in the barn. This barn was replaced by a conventional gambrel roof barn which stands today. There is no evidence of this barn's existence since the area where it was located is now occupied by a cattle yard. The old barn was located just north and east of the existing barn. Much of this information was obtained from Eugene Sobek and Jacob Johns.

Oscar Bundy -- Winona Township
This true round barn barn was thought to have been built by Oscar Bundy. At a later time a rectangular barn was attached. The round barn had a tiled silo in the middle. This barn stood for over 70 years and was torn down when the Winona Vocational Technical school was built on its grounds. A street in the area is named after Bundy.

Hans Schott -- Warren Township
This barn is said to have been built in 1913 and is documented with a photograph and eye witness accounts. The farm was subsequently owned by Evan Zander and the farm where the barn stood is now owned by Daryl Schwantz. The original road went through the farm

yard immediately next to the round barn. The road was moved further to the south. According to Daryl Schwantz, the barn came down in the fall of 1980 after a wind storm that summer. Essentially the barn had begun to "steamrot" from moisture and was unusable in its later years. The barn was 60 feet in diameter, had no silo and one grain bin. The barn was "cabled" in the 1950's to keep it from splitting open.

Roth -- St Charles Township -- George Roth Farm

The existence of this barn has not been confirmed. This barn is said to have existed on the north side of US Highway 14, just west of Utica. Marguerite (Keller) Brogan remembers seeing this barn which is said to have been destroyed by a tornado in 1926. Mrs. Brogan remembers that the barn was lifted off its foundation exposing the hay inside. She remembers driving to see the barn on the day after the storm.

Mueller or Miller

The existence of this barn also has not been confirmed. Mrs. Brogan remembers seeing this barn which is also said to have been destroyed by a tornado in 1926. Mrs. Brogan remembers that there were two round barns between St. Charles and Utica on the north side of the road, and that both barns were lifted off their foundations by the storm.

Martin Gallager

Refer to page seven.

Jim Heinlen's work depicts these farm buildings in their natural setting. The barns were made of native building materials including sand for mortar, foundation stone, and locally cut lumber. Most books provide a black and white photo of a round or polygonal barn and then present it in its context of the overall round barn phenomena. This type of treatment does not capture the reader's attention or imagination as does a full color painted detailed farm scene. A detailed appendix containing photographic inventory in black and white photos (usually 1.5 inches by 2 inches) can document these structures but will not elevate these structures to the level needed to save them. Their beauty can only be captured as an art form.

Jim Heinlen has completed at least 60 paintings of the area's round and polygonal barns in Winona County, Olmsted County, Wabasha County, Goodhue County, Fillmore County, and other parts of Minnesota. He has also painted round barns in Wisconsin and Iowa. His paintings are the primary record of these historic structures. Saint Mary's University of Minnesota has a collection of many of Jim Heinlen's round barn paintings on permanent display in its Fitzgerald library which may be viewed by the general public by appointment with the library.

Preservation of Barns

Barn preservation has significantly grown as barn owners realize the significance of these structures and their adaptive reuse for other purposes. While it is too late for many round barns, there is now a wide array of information on barn saving efforts on the national scale as well as programs from several Midwest states that include the National Trust for Historic Preservation "Barn Again" Program, and the National Register of Historic Places which provides possible tax credit programs, assistance with finding skilled craftsmen, and reuses for farming, housing, and hunting camps.

The Round Barns of Winona County, Minnesota, and Environs

Table of Contents

While there are many texts on the subject of barn reuse and preservation, most present arguments for preservation at the end of the book. Both Ohio and Indiana have state programs patterned after the "Barn Again" program of the National Trust for Historic Preservation and an effort should be explored to initiate a program in Minnesota. The Wisconsin State Historical Society conducts several barn preservation workshops each year. Just as an inventory in tiny format serves to document the past, Jim Heinlen's art work can fortify the recognition that these structures are sadly being lost forever.

1 Gallagher	Page 11
2 Pfeiffer - Dabelstein	Page 12
3 Heublein	Page 14
4 Molstein - Agrimson	Page 15
5 Nichols	Page 16
6 Keller - Brogan	Page 17
7 Feltes - Biers	Page 18
8 Hilke - Kalmes	Page 19
9 Prudohel - Rupprecht	Page 20
10 Meisch	Page 22
11 Ries - Turbiest or Terbeest - Meyer	Page 23
12 Speltz - Anderson - Kronebusch	Page 24
13 Walsh - Greden - Ellinghuysen	Page 26
14 Speltz - Lowenhagen - Bolduan	Page 27
15 Kirch - Maus - Mueller - Ahrens/Lafky	Page 28
16 Tibesar	Page 30
17 Ames - Marx	Page 31
18 Murray	Page 32
19 Lejk or Laak	Page 33
20 Church	Page 34

The Round Barns of Winona County, Minnesota, and Environs

Map of Winona County, Minnesota

★ - Barn standing
● - Barn gone

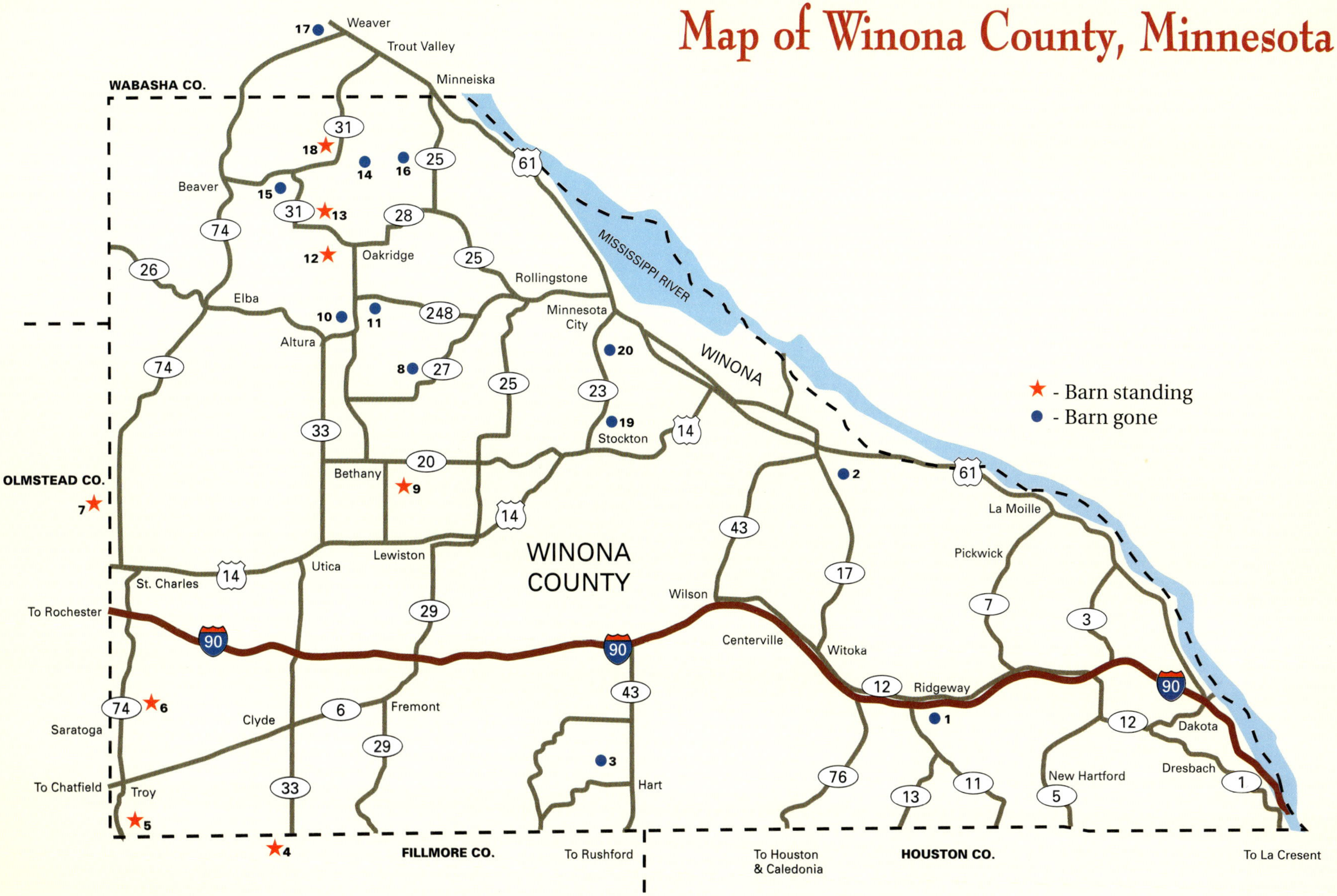

This Old Barn

*If you listen closely now,
You still might hear the sounds
Echoing around in this old barn
Of neighing horse, or mooing cow,
Or the farmer as he calls
Returning from his labor
In the field, at the plow.*

*Lingers too in this old barn
The musty scent of hay
Way up to the rafters, once was stored
And the pungent smell of animals
Or sweaty children hard at play
Helping father with the chores
On a golden summer's day.*

*In its prime this old barn
Brushed red with paint till it shined
Onto boards newly sawed
Within the builder's plan
With care were squarely placed
Onto a strong foundation base
Of stone, cut and quarried. all by hand.*

*This old barn though weathered now
Still stands proud and tall,
Though no farmer finds it useful
And only pigeons come to call.
Its nostalgic beauty lasts
Till the final storm doth pass
Claiming this old barn, once and for all.*

Joan Murphy
Winona, MN

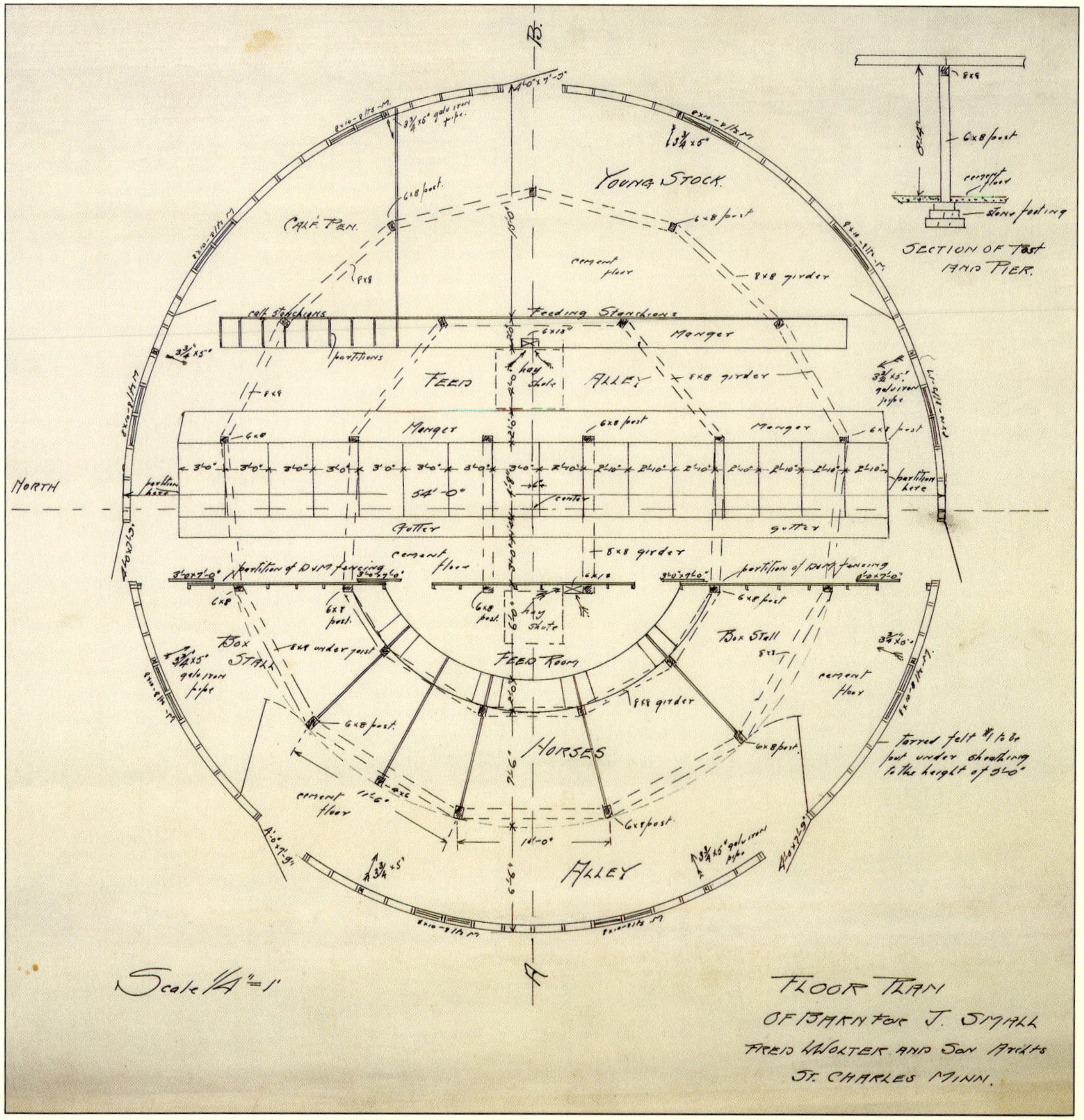

Small barn, lower level floor plan showing livestock areas and stanchions for 16 cows.

Martin Gallagher
-- Pleasant Hill Township -- True Round Barn

This barn was located south of Interstate 90 just south of Ridgeway on the north side of Winona County Highway 8 and east of Winona County Highway 11. The barn was located west of a gravel township road on what is now the Gordon Gerdes Farm. A photo of this barn was obtained from Mr. Gerdes and from Angela Gallagher Dumond which was used for this painting. The barn is unusual in that it contains four dormer windows and a massive cupola. The photo shows the barn with vertical siding and a fieldstone foundation. The barn had windows in the upper mow area as well. The photo contains three horses and a person standing in front of the barn. This barn is said to have been used for dances in the spring when it was empty. The barn is said to have had a maple floor. Money collected at the dances was used as a fundraiser for the nearby St. Patrick's Catholic Church. The barn is thought to have been built in 1905 and burned down mysteriously in 1926. It is said that the owner heard a car leaving the farm late one night after a dance and it is suspected that this person(s) burned it down. The barn was replaced by a rectangular structure. All that remains is the elevated driveway where the milkhouse would have been. The driveway leads to the new barn.

Angela Gallagher Dumond remembered that the barn was once painted blue.

The Round Barns of Winona County, Minnesota, and Environs

Stone masons, hauling stones up via wheelbarrow to construct the silo.

Pfeiffer - Dabelstein
-- Homer Township -- Octagonal Barn

Mr. Clint Dabelstein purchased the farm from Pfeiffer in 1947 and sold it in 1977. This barn was constructed in 1915 and was located in Pleasant Valley west of Winona County Highway 17 approximately two miles south of the intersection with State Highway 43 (south). The barn was located in what is now Valley Estates on the east side of the subdivision. Nothing remains of this barn, which was painted red, contained a silo and had a small rectangular barn behind it. This barn could have been restored and incorporated into the subdivision as perhaps a community center. Many newer suburban developments are now keeping the old farm buildings as the identifying feature of the development.

Jim's grandfather crashed this party. Can you find him?

12

The Round Barns of Winona County, Minnesota, and Environs

This was originally known as the Evergreen Farms round barn in Pleasant Valley.

The Round Barns of Winona County, Minnesota, and Environs

A deserted building, pioneer built, now in ruins. It had a beautiful lavender-like patina on the weathered wood siding and a wonderful red, almost orange, patch roof. The top of the cupola was gone with the wind.

Heublein

-- Hart Township -- True Round Barn

This barn was located about one mile west of Highway 43 and one mile south of Interstate 90. The farmstead is abandoned now, yet many of the buildings were still standing. All that remains of this barn is the lower level with the roof collapsed. The lower level barn was still in fine shape and contained wood that someone had intended to store there. This barn had a unique center pillar made of native foundation stone. The pillar has a diameter of approximately four feet. All of the main floor joists centered on this pillar. No other barns encountered had this feature. In looking in the house, an original portion was found to consist of a log cabin. The whole farmstead is abandoned and now is littered with old junk autos and machinery.

Art Molstein - Agrimson
-- Fillmore County -- True Round Barn

This barn is located south of Utica in Fillmore County approximately 1/2 mile south of the Winona County line. The barn can be reached by following Winona County Highway 33 south from Utica toward Minnesota State Highway 30. Highway 30 is the road between Chatfield and Rushford. This barn is a big white barn approximately 70 feet in diameter. The barn contains a wooden silo. The barn is used for hay storage. The lower level was not used. The barn, said to have cost $1800 to build, needs a new roof soon.

This is the neatest place, an absolutely immaculate farm run by a very fine bachelor farmer. The painting was from an old photo Art had when the cupola was still up. Note the two little relatives returned from Sunday school - white shirts and ties - shades of the 1930's! The cupola came down later.

The Round Barns of Winona County, Minnesota, and Environs

Thomas & George Nichols
-- Saratoga Township -- True Round Barn

This barn is located 1.2 miles east of State Highway 74 and Winona County Highway 43. The barn is painted red and is approximately 54 feet in diameter. The original owners were ancestors of Thomas and George Nichols. The barn is said to have been built in 1906. The current owner, Mitchel Stethem, has a copy of the original barn plans. This barn did not contain a silo; the cupola, an unusually high structure, is still intact. The barn is no longer used but was in use until the Stethems bought the property 10 years ago. The house used to be a stage coach stop and was an inn and a tavern.

This wonderful barn has an unusually tall cupola. Bachelor brothers Herb and Tom worked this farm which they inherited from their parents and grandparents. Herb, in the foreground, passed away later. Son Sean Heinlen is in the background.

This barn is so handsome, dignified, and well-kept. The house was added in this scene because it served as a hotel and tavern for stagecoaches passing through during the 1850's. Wood frame in structure, it is now stuccoed.

16

Adolph Keller - Brogan
-- Saratoga Township -- True Round Barn

The siding of this barn has been replaced with sheet metal and the old cupola has been replaced by a modern metal stack. The red buildings are typical of the newer farm buildings.

This barn is located approximately 4.6 miles south of St. Charles off State Highway 74 on the north side of a gravel township road and approximately 1/4 mile north and east of Saratoga. The original owner was Adolph Keller (Marguerite Brogan's father). The barn was built in 1910 by Frederick Wolter of St. Charles but burned down in 1911. Mr. Keller hauled the sand for the foundation material from the Root River (8 miles) by wagon and the wood for the barn was cut on the farm and was hand hewed. The barn was rebuilt in 1911 and was in use as a dairy barn until 1981. It had room for 37 cows on the outside and nine in the center. In 1947, the Brogans installed a one-track barn cleaner and in the 1960's put on a new roof for $3,600. The wooden shingles were replaced by asphalt shingles. There is galvanized steel siding which covered the horizontal wood siding. In 1922, the cupola blew off and was replaced. In 1960 the cupola tipped. The barn is currently used for dry cows and has a granary in the hay mow. The diameter is approximately 62 feet. Marguerite Brogan has written several short stories about the round barn titled "In the Shadows of the Round Barn," "If the Round Barn Could Talk," "Let Barn Tell Whole Story."

The Round Barns of Winona County, Minnesota, and Environs

This barn is located about three miles northwest of St. Charles. Although the original siding was replaced by metal, the old, beautiful cupola still dignifies this barn.

Feltes - Leonard Biers
-- Olmsted County -- True Round Barn

This barn is located approximately one mile west of the Winona County line into Olmsted County and approximately 3/4 of a mile north of Olmsted County Highway 9 on County Road 107. The barn is located on the west side of the road. The barn was also designed and built by Frederick Wolter of St. Charles, Minnesota, in 1904. The owner was Charles Feltes who was Leonard Biers' grandfather. The barn is covered by grey metal siding. It has the original wood shingled roof which is showing signs of its age. Mr. Biers has said that a new roof would cost $30,000. The barn is currently used for beef cows and hay storage. The barn has a fieldstone foundation, a small cupola and a small granary in the upper mow. The diameter is approximately 60 feet and the barn is approximately 52 feet in height. Mr. Biers stated that the wood was hauled to the site on box cars from Wisconsin.

Hilke - Eugene Kalmes
-- Norton Township -- True Round Barn.

This barn was destroyed by wind in June of 1998. It was located southwest of Rollingstone on Winona County 27 approximately 3.5 miles south and west of State Highway 248. This barn is said to have been built in 1916. It had the original tin siding which was painted in the 1940's. Prior to its recent demise, the barn was used for storage and as a calf barn. There was a silo in the middle made out of yellow pine. At the time the barn came down there was no cupola.

A violent storm took off the roof and spun it like a frisbee onto the farm yard on June 27, 1998.

The red barn was painted white in later years.

The Round Barns of Winona County, Minnesota, and Environs

Prudohel - Rupprecht
-- Utica Township -- True Round Barn

This barn is located south of Bethany. From Bethany go south on Winona County Highway 20 to the T - intersection, go right (west) on town road to the first intersection, go left (south) to first gravel road on left, go left (east) to the barn on the north side of the road. This barn is unused and is approximately 60 feet in diameter. A faded red with vertical siding, the barn has all of the stanchions still in place and contains the track cable system for feeding the livestock.

The Round Barns of Winona County, Minnesota, and Environs

This painting graces the cover of this book as well as the wall of Prime Steak and Cake restaurant in Winona. The little red cardinal is as beautiful as the barn and farmstead.

The Round Barns of Winona County, Minnesota, and Environs

John Meisch
-- Norton Township -- True Round Barn

The Meisch barn was located on Minnesota State Highway 248 between Rollingstone and Altura (approximately one mile from Altura). The barn was quite visible as it was located at a bend in the road. Said to have been built in 1908, the barn originally had room for 18 milk cows. The lower barn was gutted in 1949 in order to house 40 cows. The barn did contain a silo. In more recent times, the upper barn was used to store machinery. According to Peggy Starck's article in the Winona County Historical Society's "Chronicle," 1983, the barn was renovated in 1949, but it was too expensive to repair and maintain and too inefficient for modern farming practices.

The prominent white structure was seen as quite impractical by the owner even soon after it was built. This wonderful small barn with metal replacement siding was razed many years ago. The doors were painted red to add a bit of color.

The Round Barns of Winona County, Minnesota, and Environs

Ries - Turbiest or Terbeest - Meyer
-- Norton Township -- True Round Barn

This barn was located at the top of "straight valley" on Minnesota State Highway 248 on the south side of the road, just before Winona County Highway 31. This barn was thought to have been built in 1910. The roof was blown off in 1949 and was replaced by a dome type roof (rather than having a roof with sides). This barn was rather unusual in that its silo protruded through the roof of the barn. There is no evidence of this barn, as it was removed and replaced by a modern dairy operation.

This was quite an unusual barn in that the roof starts from the stone foundation rather than the sides, which is the usual case. The silo also comes straight through the roof and perhaps replaced an older one. The arched ribbing inside the barn is architecturally awesome.

I couldn't resist painting this view because of the funny, interesting shed to the left and the beautiful hay stacks.

The Round Barns of Winona County, Minnesota, and Environs

Louis Speltz -Anderson-Kronebusch

-- Mount Vernon Township -- True Round Barn

This barn is located on Township Road 114, 1/2 mile west of Winona County Highway 31 and north of State Highway 248. This barn had been converted to a calf barn, but recently its use for that purpose is diminishing. The barn remains in use since the milkhouse and milking parlor were added. Most other barns were converted for young livestock whereas this barn is the best example of adaptation into a more modern dairy function. There is a wooden granary in the hay loft rather than a silo. This barn has an asphalt shingled roof which needs replacing. The owner, Leroy Kronebusch, estimates the cost of a new roof at $30,000. This barn is much larger than the Murray barn (as well as most other round barns in the county) with an approximate diameter of 80 feet. This barn has a stone foundation. A painting of this barn by Jim is in the Rochester dental office of Dr. Ken Sak, a round barn advocate in his own right.

24

The Round Barns of Winona County, Minnesota, and Environs

The fields are still golden, but dusted with snow. I love to paint "ridge" scenes.

The Round Barns of Winona County, Minnesota, and Environs

Around the bend provided a beautiful view with the school bus chugging up the road.

Edward Walsh - Greden - Ellinghuysen
-- Mount Vernon Township -- True Round Barn

This barn is located on Winona County Highway 31, approximately two miles north of State Highway 248. This barn is located on the north side of the road in the heart of the historic village of Oak Ridge and just north of the Catholic Church. The barn is painted white (was red at one time) with vertical metal siding. The foundation is stone with some cinder block. The barn is probably the best maintained of all of the remaining barns.

This barn is next to Immaculate Conception Church, which adds to the air of serenity. The church, unfortunately, was recently closed. The cow on the rise and the cupola in red add wit and dash to the white barn.

J. P. Speltz - Lowenhagen - Bolduan

-- Mount Vernon Township -- True Round Barn

This barn was located at the end of Mount Vernon Township Road 5 south of Minneiska off Winona County Highway 25. The barn was thought to have been built in 1905. The barn was in full use as a dairy barn until 1977-78 and then was converted to a calf barn; in 1991 it blew down. The barn was also used for hay storage until that time. The wind twisted the barn and split it open on the west side (the outside boards ripped away). Even though the barn was "split open," it was used as a calf barn until it came completely down. It contained a cupola, wood silo and a stone foundation. The barn is still visible as a pile of rubble with the owners salvaging the wood.

Farmer Paul loved his round barn and loved to talk about it. The barn is down now, ripped apart in a storm and later razed after I painted this picture.

The horizontal siding, denoting a very old barn, had a shiny quality. The new modern barn lent a sharp contrast to the old.

The Round Barns of Winona County, Minnesota, and Environs

Note how the silo was a structural component of the roof in this early construction photo.

Michael Kirch - Maus - Mueller - Ahrens/Lafky
-- Mount Vernon Township -- True Round Barn

This barn was located on Winona County 31 approximately six miles north and west of the original village of Oak Ridge, Minnesota. It is said to have been built by local builders from Rollingstone, Minnesota, for Michael Kirch in 1913. The round barn contained a silo in the center which was removed in the early 1980's. Once the silo was removed, the barn began to collapse and is now only a rubble pile. It is only properly documented through Jim Heinlen's paintings and with this photo taken during its construction (featured in Winona County Historical Society's "Chronicle," 1983).

The Round Barns of Winona County, Minnesota, and Environs

This old barn had lost its original siding, which was replaced by an odd building material in large sheets. The barn was in bad shape and soon collapsed. The remains are still there.

I just had to do another painting in order to better depict that crazy Volkswagen, painted yellow and orange-red. The roof of this barn had aged to a beautiful shade of red.

The Round Barns of Winona County, Minnesota, and Environs

A violent tornado-like storm flattened this vertical sided barn years ago.

Le Roy Tibesar
-- Mount Vernon Township -- True Round Barn

This barn was located near the end of Mount Vernon Township Road 5 west of Winona County Highway 25. The barn was located on the south side of the road and just up the road from the Lowenhagen-Bolduan barn. It came down in 1985. There is some debate whether this barn was lost to lightning or heavy winds/rain. It was a large white barn surrounded by a milking parlor and other sheds and barns. Although recently sold, the farm had been in the Tibesar family for several generations. The foundation was thought to be concrete block. It is not known whether the barn had a silo.

Ames - Marx
-- Wabasha County -- Hexagonal Barn

This barn was located on Minnesota State Highway 74 approximately 3/4 of a mile south of Weaver. It is difficult to distinguish where the farmstead was as all of the buildings were torn down by a contractor on behalf of the DNR; this property is now part of the Whitewater Wildlife Management Area. The main distinguishing feature is a pine grove on the west side of the road adjacent to a field driveway. The farm buildings were all on the west side of the road. The farm actually had two barns, one hexagonal and one

This old barn collapsed many years ago; the barn on the left was termed the "new" barn, although some 60 years old.

rectangular. The hexagonal barn was used for raising hogs. The Ames' raised purebred hogs and used the barn as a sales barn. Hogs were shipped by rail from Weaver. The red dairy barn (new barn) housed Guernsey cows. This barn was built when the farm was owned by Archie Ames. The farm was later purchased by the Marx family. The hexagonal barn was natural wood with horizontal siding. It had an unusually large cupola and natural stone foundation. Barn dances were often held in the early years.

John Murray Barn
-- Mount Vernon Township -- True Round Barn

This barn is located in Trout Valley on Winona County Highway 31 via Wabasha County Highway 29, on the north side of the road approximately four miles south of Highway 61. The current owner is Gary Bauer who uses the barn for miscellaneous storage. The barn is red with horizontal siding with a stone foundation. The cupola is leaning and the foundation is cracking and the structure appears to be twisting. This barn does not contain a silo. The barn roof consists of wood shingles which need replacement. Mr. Bauer indicated that the cost of a new roof would be $15,000. Jim has painted this barn several times and painted it for Janet Murray, a direct descendant.

A beautiful round barn in beautiful Trout Valley.

The Round Barns of Winona County, Minnesota, and Environs

Lejk or Laak
-- Hillsdale Township -- True Round Barn

This barn was located just north of Stockton and U.S. Highway 14 on Winona County 23 The barn was painted white. This is the first barn that Jim Heinlen painted. Jim's wife Nora liked it so much that she suggested that Jim paint all the round barns in Winona County, so he did. This barn was gone by 1986.

This was the first round barn I painted. This was a beautiful large classic barn near Stockton. I did this double view on one sheet of paper to show it from both the south and north. It went down 15 to 20 years ago.

The Round Barns of Winona County, Minnesota, and Environs

Russell and Ried Church
-- Rollingstone Township -- True Round Barn

This barn too was located just north of Stockton on Winona County 23 about a mile north of U.S. Highway 14. Located north of the Laak barn, this barn sat where a pole shed stands today. The barn was a large "handsome" barn with weathered grey horizontal wood siding, with a silo inside and a stone foundation. The interior wood was cottonwood.

Under construction many years ago.

Between the tall pines, a beautiful round barn.

The Round Barns of Winona County, Minnesota, and Environs

Of course I had to do a snow scene of the whole valley.

The barn is gone. When I painted it, the bright red had faded and worn to produce a natural wood pinkish-grey patina.

The Round Barns of Winona County, Minnesota, and Environs

The Round Barn
by Edna Lovelace, *Poems for Every Day*

A round barn on a farm is a real rarity,
It's something a traveler does not often see;
But there are a few in the country I've found,
Though most barns are square or oblong, not round.

I don't know the reason why they're built that way;
The cows surely don't care which way they eat hay,
With their heads to the center or to the outside,
It's up to the farmer, I guess, to decide.

The farmer, perhaps, puts a big bale of hay
Right there in the middle and calls it a day
Until the time comes for the barn to be cleaned,
Then the way to is around, it would seem.

Most farmers prefer a rectangular shape,
And that is the kind they usually make,
But it's nice, as we travel the country, to see
A round barn on a farm that's a real rarity.

Hans Schott round barn near The Arches, Warren Township, built in 1913, torn down in 1980. Early photo.

Design: Kathrine S. Myrah
Print Coordination: Jessica E. Smith
Production Coordination: Jim Heinlen
Typeface: Utopia
Printed on 80# Moistrite Matte enamel text

November 4, 1998

Printed at Winona Printing Company
Winona, Minnesota
USA